ANCIENT CHINESE EMPERORS AND HOW THEY RULED

CHILDREN'S ANCIENT HISTORY BOOKS

BABY PROFESSOR

EDUCATION KIDS

Speedy Publishing LLC
40 E. Main St. #1156
Newark, DE 19711
www.speedypublishing.com
Copyright 2016

Let's learn about
Ancient China.

For a long period,
China was ruled
by powerful
groups of families
called Dynasties.

The Shang
dynasty was the
first to rule and
the Qing dynasty
was the last.

Among the empires in the world, the Chinese Empire lasted the longest, enduring for more than 2000 years. It started in 221 BC with Emperor Qin as the first emperor who united China.

Before the time
of the empires,
the Chinese
people followed
the feudal system
in which local
lords owned
their own lands
and had farmers
plant for them
and serve them
in other ways.

However, when the system of government was changed with the rise of the empires, there were then civil service officials who enforced laws, ruled the cities, and collected taxes. These officials had to pass an exam to qualify for their positions.

How was the
emperor chosen?

皇建有極
天心降鑒惟萬方臣庶

When the emperor died, his oldest son would normally be the next emperor. However, there were times that people who wanted to take over caused a war as they tried to get the throne.

Here are some
of the most
famous emperors
of China.

Qin Shi Huang, who was the first emperor, founded the Qin Dynasty. He started many political and economic reforms, and built the Great Wall of China. When he died, the whole Terracotta Army was buried with him. He ruled from 221 BC to 210 BC.

Emperor Gaozu of the Han Dynasty was a peasant before he became an emperor. He helped in leading the fight to defeat the Qin Dynasty.

祾恩殿
景区内 Scenic Spots
严禁吸烟 Refuse Smoking

When his side won, he became the leader and became the first emperor of the Han Dynasty.

He made
Confucianism
part of the
Chinese
government
and lowered
the tax rate. He
ruled from 202
BC to 195 BC.

先師孔子行教像
韓喜爽捐刻

Emperor Wu of the Han Dynasty ruled China for 57 yrs from 141 BC to 87 BC. He expanded China by many military campaigns. He established a strong, centralized government and helped improve the arts, especially music and poetry.

Emperor Taizong
helped in
establishing the
Tang Dynasty.
He implemented
changes in the
government and
economy that
brought into
China a golden
age of prosperity
and peace.

His time of rule was considered as the best in the history of China. He ruled from 626 AD to 649 AD.

Empress Wu Zetian is the only woman who has ruled China so far. Her officials were promoted based on their talents and not based on their family ties. She reformed the government and economy that caused China to flourish.

Kublai Khan conquered China from AD 1260 to AD 1294. He was the ruler of the Mongols. In 1271, he established the Yuan Dynasty. He established trade with people outside of China and built many public works to strengthen the nation's infrastructure.

Emperor Hongwu started the Ming Dynasty in AD 1368. He forced the Mongols out of China. He distributed land to the peasants and had a very powerful army. He also made new codes of law.

Did you enjoy reading this book? Share this to your friends.

Visit
BABY PROFESSOR
EDUCATION KIDS
www.BabyProfessorBooks.com
to download Free Baby Professor eBooks
and view our catalog of new and exciting
Children's Books

* 9 7 9 8 8 6 9 4 4 2 8 5 7 *